australia's
hidden places

To Tony, Jo and family.

Thank you so much for your care
and hospitality over the past 18 years.
Friendships that develop out of love will
always last even when distance separates.

August 2005

Alan

australia's
hidden places

nick rains

VIKING
an imprint of
PENGUIN BOOKS

for Sylvia Rains

Contents

introduction

Introduction

Australia is famous throughout the world as a land of stunning scenery. In fact Uluru is rated as one of the most recognised sights anywhere on the planet. With natural attractions like the Great Barrier Reef, Twelve Apostles, Kakadu and the Daintree Rainforest, there is a veritable feast of experiences to be had. It is tempting for any photographic book on Australia to concentrate on these destinations and leave out the lesser-known spots. However, in this book I deliberately avoid the best-known places, choosing instead to show that between the famous landmarks are others of no lesser beauty, that in some cases rival the popular icons. Some places you will see are very close to familiar destinations and by simply going a bit further or spending a bit more time, these little gems can be revealed.

As a landscape photographer for the past sixteen years I have, of course, portrayed the iconic places of Australia many times; their popularity and fame are clearly justified. Who could forget flying low in a helicopter over the exquisite blue lacework of Hook Reef off the far north Queensland coast, or seeing the vast red bulk of Uluru for the first time?

Like all vast continents, Australia's landscape and geology are enormously varied, so the range of scenery is almost endless. In my travels I like to explore a bit further than many visitors; I love to head down obscure roads just because they look interesting and in particular I am intrigued by names on maps. Some of my best-known images have come about simply by following my nose – always wondering what's around the next corner, and then finding out.

Over the years I have found some treasures; in fact many of the places in this book I wish I could visit again for the first time. I have clear and valued memories of finding Karijini National Park in the Northern Territory, back in 1997. Among its many remarkble formations is a startling little gorge with abrupt towering walls – and you need to swim to get there, a fact that puts many people off. However, if you do make the effort the rewards are there for the taking, as I hope my images will show.

A classic example of Australia's hidden places is secreted within the Blue Mountains National Park in New South Wales. Katoomba is considered the heart of the Blue Mountains and is only 90 minutes drive from Sydney. The Blue Mountains are one of the most visited places in the country, with the Three Sisters, Wentworth Falls and Govett's Leap receiving vast numbers of visitors every day. The view over the Jamieson Valley at the Three Sisters lookout is sensational, so it's not surprising it is so popular.

But look a little closer – what about the Valley of the Waters, right next to Wentworth Falls, or the Grand Canyon? These are not easy walks – both have steep descents and take about three hours to complete – but they are among the most spectacular places in Australia. The Grand Canyon in particular is a challenging loop walk through narrow canyons, but it never seems to be busy and each time I have been there it is hard to believe I am only two hours from the heart of metropolitan Sydney.

In Victoria is the little known Tarra Bulga National Park. For classic temperate rainforest, patterned with the swirling branches of huge tree ferns, you would be hard-pressed to find a better spot. Yet it is only about 200 km east of the city, most of which is an easy drive along the freeway. Tarra Bulga is about 25 km south of the main Princes Highway and so most travellers simply miss it on their way to or from Melbourne.

That's what this book is all about – the places that are easily missed, the places that are simply not well known, and the places that are a bit harder to get to. But you don't require a fully equipped convoy of Land Cruisers or a team of Sherpas to get to them. Some may be quite a distance from the city, but others are right under your feet. Best of all, because many of the places you will see in this book are a little harder to get to, or take a little more time to reach, the chances of having them all to yourself are that much greater.

I am fortunate to have been able to visit the places in this book. I hope my images will inspire you to do the same.

Happy exploring.
Nick Rains

alpine national park

Alpine National Park (VIC)

This is Victoria's largest national park, covering 646 000 hectares of wild high country, sparkling rivers and high plateaus. In the summer it is a fabulous place to camp, bushwalk and explore by four-wheel-drive. In the winter the deep snow makes it a Mecca for cross-country skiers, who can traverse long distances staying overnight in the original cattlemen's huts scattered throughout the region.

One of the most striking aspects of this part of Victoria has to be the sense of remoteness that you feel here. The views from The Bluff and Mt Stirling seem to go on forever, with hazy blue ridges marching to the horizon. From some of the highest points you can even see the curvature of the Earth and the feeling of being so small in such a vast open space can be quite exhilarating.

Around Falls Creek, on the Bogong High Plains, are some of the best snow gums in the area and the iconic Wallace's Hut nestles amongst them in a sheltered hollow. In the summer you can get there by car and it's an easy walk to the hut. In winter this is a favourite destination for cross-country skiers.

To the south-west of Falls Creek is the secluded Wonnangatta Valley, with the river of the same name meandering through. In the summer this is a great place to camp, fish and walk but you will need a decent four-wheel-drive vehicle since the roads are unmaintained and can be very slow.

Further west, and a bit easier to get to, is Mt Stirling, made famous by the movie *The Man from Snowy River*. The set built for the movie still exists here and has become an icon of the area – Craig's Hut is the quintessential cattleman's hut, with views of valley after valley heading to infinity.

If fishing is your thing, some of the best trout streams in the country flow through this area. Mention the Howqua, the King or the Mitta Mitta rivers to a keen fly-fisher and they will go all misty-eyed at the thought of such perfect streams, not to mention the pan-sized trout found within.

The high country is something of a legend, but one you can enjoy for yourself. There are plenty of places to visit by car and the variety of scenery has to be seen to be believed.

How to get there: Falls Creek is about 375 km from Melbourne; the trip takes 3–5 hours. Mt Stirling is accessed from Mansfield and Falls Creek is accessed from Bright.

Best time: Summer for bushwalking and camping, winter for skiing.

Facilities: Most of the ski resorts have full facilities such as camping, shops, fuel, etc.

Nearest towns: Mansfield, Bright, Myrtleford, Omeo.

Website: www.parkweb.vic.gov.au (downloadable park brochure)

bay of fires and
the north-east

Bay of Fires and the north-east (TAS)

Like all parts of Australia, Tasmania has its iconic locations, such as Cradle Mountain, Strahan, Hobart, Port Arthur, and so on. And, also like other places, there are regions that people tend to pass by due to hectic touring schedules or simply because they aren't aware that these gems are there.

East of Launceston is a very interesting part of the state, stretching from the peaceful villages of the north coast, through the Tamar Valley wineries and across a mountainous region of thick rainforest to the coast near St Helens.

Bridport on the north coast is a seemingly untouched fishing village with some excellent beaches and, unusually these days, a council-run camping ground right on the beach. The village is very popular with holidaying families and has a certain nostalgic feel about it – everywhere you look there are families out walking, swimming and picnicking. There is a peaceful little river harbour with a few moored wooden boats, and the pace of life seems a bit slower.

Heading south-east towards the coast, the road winds up over a mountain pass through thick stands of myrtle beeches festooned with 'old man's beard', a variety of clematis; if the clouds are low, the misty shapes of the trees are like something out of *The Lord of the Rings*.

Travelling down to St Helens you will go past the turnoff to St Columba Falls, which is a worthwhile detour to see not only the delightful waterfall but also a gorgeous trail passing under a canopy of ancient tree ferns and over little brooks inhabited by small trout. It is easy to imagine that this is what much of Tasmania was like thousands of years ago.

Not far from St Helens is the coastal village of Binalong Bay, the gateway to the Bay of Fires. The coast here is scattered with huge boulders decked out with intensely orange lichen that makes a striking contrast to the blue sky and the blue waters of the Tasman Sea. The beaches are delightful and with the north-eastern cape being completely untouched there are extensive walks to be enjoyed, including some multi-day hikes.

The Bay of Fires Lodge, which caters for visitors, is the only building for 20 km. The guided walk offered by the lodge takes four days and is fast becoming one of the great walks of Australia, along with the Cradle Mountain to Lake St Clair walk in the south-west.

How to get there: St Helens is 170 km east of Launceston.

Best Time: Spring through to autumn. Winter is cold and can be wet.
Weather is very changeable here, so always bring woollies!

Facilities: Places to stay at Bridport, St Helens, Binalong Bay.

Nearest towns: St Helens, Scottsdale.

Website: www.tourtasmania.com

bellinger river valley

Bellinger River Valley (NSW)

Bellingen village, set back just a few kilometres from the coast, is a good place to start exploring the beautiful Bellinger River National Park and the Dorrigo Plateau above.

Just outside the village is one of the most pleasant little rivers I have come across. The evocatively named Never Never Creek winds its way through the forest and is crossed numerous times by Promised Land Road. At the crossings are pebbly beaches with crystal-clear water sparkling in the sunshine. There are plenty of deep swimming holes to enjoy and the water can be quite chilly – perfect on a hot summer day.

Heading inland towards Dorrigo, the road sweeps through lush green fields and up a long climb to the plateau. Make sure you don't miss Griffith Lookout – the left-hand turnoff is at the crest of the winding hill and it's like being on top of the world. At dawn, the valley below may be filled with mist. On a clear day, you can see right down to Macksville on the coast, a good 40 km away.

A few kilometres beyond the lookout turnoff, back on the main road, is the short road to Dorrigo National Park, one of Australia's most accessible World Heritage rainforest regions. The park has some superb examples of pristine subtropical rainforest, with colossal yellow carabeens towering overhead and strangler figs wrapping around tree trunks.

One walk that is particularly worthwhile, and quite easy on the legs, is the 2-km hike to Crystal Shower Falls, where you can walk right behind the waterfall. A further kilometre takes you to Tristania Falls, where a new bridge has been built to allow easier access and viewing of this delightful cascade. You can either retrace your steps to the car park from here or continue in a long loop back to the park Visitor Centre, making the whole circuit about 6 km in all.

At the Visitor Centre, don't miss the elevated boardwalk which juts out from the steep escarpment and gives a bird's eye view of the forest and valley right back down to Bellingen.

How to get there: Bellinger River National Park is about 15 km from Bellingen, which in turn is 38 km south-west of Coffs Harbour, most of the journey via the Pacific Highway.

Best time: Any time of year, though spring is best.

Facilities: Full facilities in Bellingen, Dorrigo and Coffs Harbour.

Nearest town: Bellingen, Dorrigo.

Website: www.nationalparks.nsw.gov.au

blue mountains

Blue Mountains (NSW)

The Blue Mountains, west of Sydney, are not in themselves a 'hidden place'. In fact, the Three Sisters Lookout is one of the most visited places in Australia. But there is so much more to the Blue Mountains than lookouts and waterfalls, especially if you are prepared to take on some short (but somewhat strenuous) walks.

One of the most interesting short walks in the area is the Grand Canyon, which is often overlooked on day trips to the mountains. Far below Evans Lookout, near Blackheath, a series of deep, narrow canyons penetrates deep into the huge cliffs of the Grosse Valley. The Grand Canyon Walk follows one such chasm, from below Neate's Glen right up to Evans Lookout.

It is possible to walk the canyon from either end (the total distance is 5 km, including the walk back along the road to the car park). For much of the way the walk meanders along between vertical rock walls at times up to 100 m deep and only metres apart. There is a stream which rushes past, disappearing into hidden depths at one point only to reappear later.

Be sure to look out for side canyons Not far from the steps down from Evans Lookout there is a track which heads off the main path up a secondary gorge, getting progressively narrower as it goes. There is a little scrambling to be done here, but nothing too dramatic – just take care on the mossy rocks.

I mentioned 'strenuous' earlier. It's the climb back out of the canyon that gets the knees wobbling. I would suggest starting at the Evans Lookout end and going down the steps first: the other end is less steep, although longer, and some people prefer a steady climb to a short steep one. Either way you will be pleased when you get to the top and head to one of Blackheath's many cafes for some well-deserved refreshments.

How to get there: From Katoomba, which is around 105 km north-west of Sydney, head towards Blackheath and look for the signs to Evans Lookout.

Best time: Any time of year, but cold winters and hot summers can make the harder walks more challenging.

Facilities: Full facilities in Blackheath and Katoomba.

Nearest towns: Blackheath, Katoomba.

Website: www.nationalparks.nsw.gov.au

boodjamulla national park

Boodjamulla National Park (QLD)

Boodjamulla National Park, previously known as Lawn Hill, is a long way from anywhere: it's about 340 km north-west of Mt Isa in far north Queensland. The roads are mostly unsealed, and while the area is accessible by conventional vehicle a decent four-wheel-drive is highly recommended; check with the park office for road conditions.

This is a special place. The deep waterhole right next to the camping ground is so peaceful it is tempting to go no further and just while away the days in the shade or on a floating airbed. After the dusty and bumpy journey, the clean fresh water is a tonic for the senses, and many long-distance outback tourers spend many days here recharging their batteries.

The gorge itself is best appreciated from a canoe and these can be hired by the day. It is only a short paddle up Lawn Hill Creek, around a corner and on towards the gradually steepening cliffs. Take your time (and lunch), and spend the day on the water, enjoying the echoes of each stroke bouncing from the steep red walls.

About a kilometre down the river there is a remarkable feature, The Cascades, where a natural weir has developed and created a string of small waterfalls across the gorge itself. You can walk or canoe to this spot for a refreshing swim and shower under the little falls while you watch the birds dip and flit from one rock to another. It is possible to take your canoe above the cascades to the upper gorge, via a clever wooden ramp with built-in rollers so you can slide your boat easily up the incline. It's only a few metres and the upper gorge is well worth the effort.

Camping is limited and can be booked in advance through the National Parks website. In fact, it is a good idea to check in advance whatever the time of year, because you will not be allowed to camp here if all the sites are taken. Fortunately there is extra camping at nearby Adels Grove.

There are plenty of well-defined walking trails in the park, from 10-minute loops to four-hour treks to the upper gorge. If you do any of the walks, make sure you take water with you because it can be very hot at any time of year.

The campsite abounds with wildlife, as this is an oasis in an otherwise inhospitable part of the country. The creek is home to archerfish and freshwater turtles, and in the bushes red-winged parrots and purple-crowned fairy wrens can often be spied.

How to get there: Boodjamulla National Park is 90 km west of Gregory Downs on the Matilda Highway from Cloncurry to Normanton. There is also access from the Barkly Highway, 71 km east of Camooweal.

Best time: Roads are often closed in the hot wet season (December–March). Dry but cold nights in the dry season. Spring and autumn are usually perfect.

Facilities: Camping ground (bookings essential), canoe hire. Fuel at Adels Grove.

Nearest towns: Mt Isa, Camooweal.

Website: www.epa.qld.gov.au

brindle creek

Brindle Creek (NSW)

The Border Ranges National Park is a section of the World Heritage-listed south-eastern rainforests and runs along the border of New South Wales and Queensland. This is a wild and rugged part of the Great Dividing Range and is generally bypassed by the main roads in the region, which is why the little jewel that is Brindle Creek is hardly ever heard of.

Like its more famous cousin, Lamington National Park, this region is quite elevated, in parts reaching well over 1000 m above sea-level. This, together with high rainfall, makes the area ideal for the ancient Antarctic beech, which can be seen along the Brindle Creek Walking Trail.

This is nature at its most heady. Every surface is covered in damp moss, vines hang from colossal cedar trees and the falling rain muffles sound, giving you a sense of being in another world.

The park feels and looks remote, but fortunately this is one of the more accessible parts of the temperate rainforest and a well-maintained one-way loop track takes you to within metres of the best spots. The more adventurous can brave the 5-km walk from the Brindle Creek picnic area to the Antarctic beech picnic area, passing Selva Falls on the way. This is one of the better walks in the region – not too far, but far enough to give a sense of achievement at the end and a genuine feeling of how this region has not changed over thousands of years.

Further around the loop is the Pinnacle walk, a short track to a lookout with a sensational view east towards Mt Warning and the Tweed Valley. On a clear day you can see to the coast, and on a showery day you can sometimes see the rain sweeping across the valley in spectacular sheets.

Like many places, Brindle Creek is lovely in fine weather. However, as a photographer, I find that sometimes a location reveals its true character on a wild day – if you're willing to brave the elements, this is when the rewards can be the greatest.

How to get there: From Kyogle head 15 km north up the Summerland Way to Wiangaree, then turn right into Lynch's Creek Road. Follow signs from here.

Best time: Spring and autumn. It can be very cold in winter, but is generally good all year round, especially after rain.

Facilities: Camping, toilets, walking trails.

Nearest towns: Kyogle, Lismore.

Website: www.nationalparks.nsw.gov.au

cape crawford
and the lost city

Cape Crawford and the Lost City (NT)

Hidden away on a private property in the depths of the Northern Territory is an amazing series of rock formations known collectively as the Lost City. Luckily for those of us who like visiting fascinating places such as this, there is a way to get there even though there are no roads or tracks.

Cape Crawford is a roadhouse settlement on the Carpentaria Highway. During the dry season, from about Easter onwards, Cape Crawford Tourism flies visitors by helicopter out to the Lost City from the helipad near the Heartbreak Hotel to a special landing site amongst the rock formations. It's only a short hop, 11 km in all, and the view is sensational from the open door of the chopper, especially if you can get on the first flight of the day, just after dawn. The rocks look like the skyscrapers of some alien city; some are wider at the top than the bottom, and seem to defy gravity.

Once you have landed among the towers there is a two-hour guided walk that threads through the columns and includes a visit to two Aboriginal art sites, and local bush tucker.

The formations are made up mostly of silica – not unlike the famous Bungle Bungle beehive rocks in Western Australia. Differential erosion has exaggerated crevices in the soft rock, resulting in these peculiar fingers of rock up to 25 m tall.

The same tour operator offers access to another local spot which you cannot get to any other way. There, Poppy's Pools offer safe swimming, and a small boat to paddle around in. By paying the modest entry fee you can be guaranteed to have the whole place pretty much to yourself, as only one group is allowed in at a time, to preserve the ecology of the location.

How to get there: Cape Crawford is 271 km east of Daly Waters, on the Carpentaria Highway.

Best time: April to October only; tours are not conducted during the Wet.

Facilities: Free camping near the helipad; otherwise accomodation is available at Borroloola on the Gulf of Carpentaria.

Nearest town: Borroloola.

Website: www.capecrawfordtourism.com.au

cape leveque

Cape Leveque (WA)

At the tip of the Dampier Peninsula, 220 km from the well-known resort of Broome, lies the little known but quite delightful Cape Leveque. Multicoloured sandstone rocks back the clean sandy beaches, the sand dunes are dotted with pandanus trees, and the local eco-resort of Kooljaman has won many awards for its well-planned layout.

Kooljaman is the local Bardi word for Cape Leveque, which was so named in 1803 by Nicolas Baudin, captain of the French ship *Geographe* after the ship's hydrographer, Pierre Leveque. The lighthouse here was automated in 1986 and the land sold to the Bardi people so they could develop it as a tourist complex.

Right from the beginning this resort was intended to be as low-key as possible and though the term 'resort' might conjure up images of high-rise hotels, nothing could be further from the truth. In fact this one is so spread out and unobtrusive that it is even hard to find! The cabins, tents and campsites are scattered amongst the dunes and connected to the central restaurant (called Dinkas) by walking trails.

There is a definite sense of 'Castaway Island' here, with long beaches to wander along and blue-green water so clear that boats seem to float in mid-air. The limited accommodation ensures that there are rarely any crowds, and the pace is kept deliberately slow to add to the relaxing atmosphere.

It is possible to fly in and out of Kooljaman, but doing so would mean missing the other interesting features of the Dampier Peninsula – the churches of Lombardina and Beagle Bay. It's hardly possible for two places of worship to be so different, from an architectural point of view. The stone church of Beagle Bay, with its traditional bell tower and whitewashed stone walls, could have been transported from a European village. Be sure to take a look inside, as the altar is hand-built from mother-of-pearl and is the only one of its kind in the world. By contrast, the church at Lombardina is of local timber, paperbark and corrugated iron – but is no less comfortable or dignified for that.

How to get there: Cape Leveque is 220 km north of Broome; a four-wheel-drive vehicle is recommended, since the main track can be quite corrugated. Air transfers can be arranged with the resort.

Best time: April to September. December–March is very hot and humid, and usually very wet.

Facilities: Full facilities at Kooljaman Resort and nearby One-Arm Point.

Nearest town: Broome.

Website: www.kooljaman.com.au

carnarvon national park

Carnarvon National Park (QLD)

Carnarvon Gorge, in Queensland's rugged central highlands, is reasonably well known, but there are actually three other sections of the Carnarvon National Park that can be visited. Salvatore Rosa is the most westerly, followed by Ka Ka Mundi to the north and Mt Moffatt not far from the main Carnarvon Gorge section. The two best sections and fortunately the easiest to access are the eastern ones – Mt Moffatt and Carnarvon Gorge.

Mt Moffatt is a bit of an adventure to get to and this makes it quite worthwhile. The roads leading in are all gravel, sometimes a bit rough, and can be closed after rain. There are also no facilities in the camping areas, so be aware that this is no day-trip destination – it's more of a small expedition!

These facts make the area a great place for peaceful camping. And with spectacular sandstone rock formations like Marlong Arch and The Chimneys scattered throughout the park, the Mt Moffatt section provides a real bush experience for those willing to make the extra effort.

The main Carnarvon Gorge section shows the grandeur of nature, with towering sandstone cliffs forming a deep ravine right into the heart of the higher plateau. It is possible to make an extended overnight walk here and camp at Big Bend, 10 km from the information centre. On the way you pass Aboriginal rock art sites and mossy gardens, and cross the creek many times.

Carnarvon Gorge is one of those places that is a shame to visit for just a day. There are loads of walks, each of which is worth spending time enjoying. The short but steep Bluff Lookout walk has amazing views back into the gorge itself and, if you can drag yourself out of bed in the pre-dawn darkness, it is a superb spot to watch the sunrise.

Back at the Takarakka camping area, the nearby creek is inhabited by platypuses and there is a deep waterhole right behind some of the campsites where you can often see them swimming by.

Spend a while here and at Mt Moffatt for a very fulfilling – if tiring – few days. At the Visitor Centre they tell you to leave behind only footprints and take away only sore feet and photographs!

How to get there: Travel 250 km north from Injune. About 45 km of good gravel road takes you to Takarakka camping ground. The Mt Moffatt section of the park is best accessed through Mitchell or Injune and is pretty rugged – check the website (below) for conditions.

Best time: Spring and autumn. It is very hot in summer, and dry with cold nights in winter.

Facilities: Cabins at the Wilderness Lodge, camping at Takarakka. Busy during school holidays.

Nearest towns: Injune or Rolleston.

Website: www.epa.qld.gov.au/parks_and_forests

cooloola national park

Cooloola National Park (QLD)

The Great Sandy National Park is generally thought of as comprising only Fraser Island, but in fact there is another part, called the Cooloola section, which is located between Rainbow Beach and Noosa on the mainland.

This part of the national park protects the headwaters of the Noosa River, a very rich ecosystem. The river is the cleanest waterway in south-east Queensland and the only one whose entire catchment area lies within a national park.

Not only is the park of great significance from an ecological point of view, it also offers a dramatic variety of scenery for exploring. On the one hand you have the vast sweep of Laguna Bay and Teewah Beach, running for almost 40 km to Double Island Point; on the other, a series of everglades and freshwater channels running north from lakes Cootharaba and Cooroibah. Between the two are coastal sandy heathlands with large areas of open forest of scribbly gums and other eucalypts.

The Noosa River is a great place to explore, and although powered craft are not allowed above Harry's Hut camping area, if you have a canoe you can explore a long way up the river, staying overnight at any of the series of fifteen camping grounds along its banks.

The ocean beach is very popular with fishermen and campers – at low tide the wide shore is dotted with surfcasters plumbing the depths of inshore gutters, waiting for a strike. At various places along the shoreline there are sections set aside for camping on a first-come first-served basis.

The eastern seaboard beaches are some of my favourite places to camp. Not only does the sound of the surf lull me into a deep sleep every night, but taking a mug of hot coffee out onto the dunes to watch the sun rise is deeply satisfying – especially for a photographer.

Most of the interior of the park is accessible in dry conditions by normal cars, but the beach is strictly four-wheel-drive only. Take care at the southern entrance to the beach at Tewantin, because the sand can get very churned up and become quite treacherous for the inexperienced driver.

How to get there: Via Kin Kin and the Cooloola Way to Harry's Hut, or via Noosa North Shore to get to the southern beach.

Best time: All year round.

Facilities: Basic camping at Harry's Hut, bush camping along the beach. As of 2006 no open camp fires are allowed at all, due to bushfire risk.

Nearest towns: Noosa to the south, Tin Can Bay to the north.

Website: www.epa.qld.gov.au

eyre peninsula

Eyre Peninsula (SA)

Travelling west from Adelaide and Port Augusta, the first worthwhile stop is often thought to be the start of the Nullarbor Plain, and Perth the next (with very little in between). The main route west on Highway 1 heads off through a series of small rural towns on its way to Ceduna; the roadside scenery is relatively ordinary and the temptation is to keep on driving.

Yet, south of the main road is a huge triangular region known as the Eyre Peninsula, extending over 200 km south to the Southern Ocean at Port Lincoln, and there are some little gems here just waiting to be discovered. The whole east coast of the peninsula is a pleasant drive, but the best scenery is at the southernmost point, around the town of Port Lincoln. Here you'll find Lincoln National Park, Coffin Bay National Park, Sleaford Bay, and Cape Carnot.

The scenic coastal drive known as Whalers Way is unusual because it is all on private property – you need to get a key from the Port Lincoln Visitor Centre to access the privately maintained road. Cape Carnot at the southern tip was named by the French explorer Louis-Claude de Freycinet in the early 1800s. Sailors have always treated this area with the utmost respect: unprotected from the Southern Ocean, the coast is pounded by ferocious storms and the jagged coastline is no place to be shipwrecked. On the eastern shoreline there is a series of blowholes and even some caves scoured into the rocky cliffs. The constant movement of the indigo-blue waves is quite hypnotic and the power of the ocean is evident in every explosion of white surf.

Somewhat more gentle, nearby Sleaford dunes offer a respite from the dramatic vistas from Whalers Way. With a four-wheel-drive vehicle you can explore right across the dunes to the coast. The beginning of the trail here has some fantastic views towards Lincoln National Park.

Further to the west, almost as you leave the peninsula and quite near Port Kenny, are the rather unusual rock formations known as Murphy's Haystacks. Technically referred to as inselbergs, these abrupt rounded outcrops are formed by erosion of the softer surrounding rocks to reveal much harder, often free-standing, granite masses. In the evening light the red lichen encrusting the outcrops makes them look as if they are glowing with heat.

How to get there: Port Lincoln is 265 km south-west of Whyalla, which itself is 74 km from Port Augusta.

Best time: Cold, wet winters make the summer the best time to visit here.

Facilities: Most towns have either motels or camping grounds.

Nearest towns: Port Lincoln, Whyalla, Ceduna.

Website: www.tep.com.au

freycinet region

Freycinet region (TAS)

Coles Bay and the lofty red peaks of the Hazards mountains will be reasonably well known to visitors to Tasmania, but there is more to see in the area than is first apparent.

Just across Great Oyster Bay, almost directly opposite Coles Bay, is a series of beaches that are mostly unnamed. These run from Triabunna all the way up to Swansea and there are often places where you can pull your car over to the side of the road. Even in the high season there is little chance of any beach being busy, or even occupied at all, and the views across to the main Freycinet Peninsula are superb.

One beach in particular caught my eye, a few kilometres south of Swansea, where a short gravel track leads down to a circular parking area. The stretch of beach just metres from the car park was one of the best I have ever seen and there was only one other occupant – a local policeman who turned up on his lunch break to do a spot of fishing.

Just north of Coles Bay is the small town of Bicheno, which has a fishing harbour and the lichen-covered rocks found along much of the coast around here. Just outside town there is a decent blowhole, which shoots water when the waves are at just the right angle. Bicheno itself is a delightful little town and makes a good stopover on the way up the coast to St Helens.

Along the main Freycinet Peninsula there is an excellent series of lookouts on the east side of the land spur. It is worth taking the time to drive over to the Cape Tourville lighthouse and explore some of the walking trails in the area. If you get up very early you will be rewarded with wonderful views that can be enjoyed in perfect solitude. The lookout at Sleepy Bay is one of the best spots.

Freycinet National Park lies just past the town of Coles Bay and whilst many people head straight up the walking track to see famous Wineglass Bay, it is worth taking a moment to explore the sheltered coves along the southern shore of Coles Bay. There are a number of tiny bays almost fully enclosed by smooth boulders, some of which make natural swimming pools with crystal-clear water. Honeymoon Bay and Parsons Cove stand out from the rest.

How to get there: Swansea is 138 km from Hobart, and Coles Bay a further 65 km.
Best time: Spring through to autumn. Winter is cold and can be wet. Weather is changeable.
Facilities: Coles Bay has full facilities including motels and caravan parks as well as the splendid Freycinet Lodge right on the bay.
Nearest town: Swansea.
Website: www.parks.tas.gov.au/natparks/freycinet/

gregory national park

Gregory National Park (NT)

Gregory National Park is a huge area of protected land close to the Western Australian border. Split into two distinct parts, the park includes the Victoria River as it flows towards the Joseph Bonaparte Gulf, and the pastoral regions on the Bullita stock route.

The smaller, eastern section of the park centres around the Victoria River Roadhouse. It is easy to spot: after driving through relatively nondescript country, you suddenly enter a valley between high sandstone cliffs which are typical of the region. The Victoria River is just next to the roadhouse and there is a sealed road leading to a boat ramp for those keen to get a hook into the famous barramundi fish.

Just past the roadhouse the road winds between towering red walls on one side and the majestic river on the other. After a few kilometres there is a small detour to the left that leads to a picnic area and this is well worth a side trip as the road winds into a side gorge flanked by high walls on the plateau areas. From the late wet season into the beginning of the Dry, the plateau is punctuated with cascades of water as the huge volume of monsoon rain drains off the high plateau to the main river below.

Bullita, the western portion of the park, is the biggest and the hardest to access: the camping areas and trails to the south of the main road are only suitable for four-wheel-drive vehicles, and in the dry season only. There is an excellent campground just off the main highway, right on the Victoria River where Big Horse Creek joins the main flow. The boat ramp offers good access to the river, so this is a great place to base yourself if you fancy some fishing.

A few kilometres on from Big Horse Creek is Gregory's Tree, a huge boab with dates carved into the trunk by explorer by Augustus Gregory to mark the arrival and departure of his North Australian Expedition in the 1850s. This is also a sacred site for the local Aboriginal people and its significance is explained on information boards beside the path.

Gregory National Park makes a very good stopover on the long haul from Katherine to Western Australia. It's well worth an overnight stay to relax and explore the local areas.

How to get there: Victoria River Roadhouse is 190 km west of Katherine, on the Victoria Highway.

Best time: April to October, although the river can be spectacular in the wet season.

Facilities: Fuel, food and accommodation at Timber Creek and Victoria River Roadhouse.

Nearest town: Timber Creek.

Website: www.nt.gov.au/nreta/parks

karijini national park

Karijini National Park (WA)

Driving through the iron-rich, rusty-red landscape of the Pilbara, it is hard to imagine that hidden beneath the spinifex-covered hills are some of the most intriguing natural formations in the whole vast continent of Australia.

Focused on a single rocky spur, four abrupt, water-eroded slot canyons converge to form a labyrinth that the sun can hardly penetrate. Cool waterholes and smooth red rocks make the gorges of Karijini a welcome refuge from the intense heat of this remote area, but the rewards are not lightly given.

Bushwalking in this region is hard on both boot and leg, steep rocky climbs tax the less fit, and in places negotiating the narrows of the canyons requires a certain degree of 'mountain goat' balance. In other places it is necessary to swim for short distances, so make sure you don't take anything that will be damaged by water.

Weano Gorge is one of the more accessible gorges in the area, with a modest climb down from the car park into a shale river bed. The gorge rapidly narrows until you can touch both sides with your outstretched arms, and a scramble of a few hundred metres leads you to the Handrail Pool. The path drops steeply here, and a steel rail has been thoughtfully added by the National Parks department so you can slip-slide down to the green pool below. The path continues but it is treacherous and thus recommended only for those with serious caving and canyoning experience.

Knox Gorge is formed on a much grander scale, with red rock walls towering up to 100 m overhead, dotted with gravity-defying fig trees growing out of impossibly small cracks. All the gorges have permanent spring water flowing through them, and Knox has stands of beautiful malaleuca trees hanging over a series of peaceful waterholes.

Hancock Gorge is the most picturesque of all, though it is hard to get into without swimming. But the effort is well worth it, because the gorge closes down into a very narrow series of passages interspersed with deep waterholes.

It is quite possible to have the whole place to yourself, even during the more popular winter months, because getting to Karijini requires a special effort. What could be more peaceful than sitting by an iridescent-green rockpool shaded from the midday heat by a graceful paperbark tree?

How to get there: Turn west off the Great Northern Highway 35 km south of the Munjina roadhouse or 165 km north-west of Newman. The park is fully signposted.
Best time: The summer is much too hot to be safe, so choose the cooler months – April to September is ideal.
Facilities: Two camping grounds, toilets with bush showers, limited water. Roads are gravel but maintained well.
Nearest towns: Newman, or Port Hedland to the north.
Website: www.calm.wa.gov.au

killarney district

Killarney district (QLD)

Between Warwick, on the main New England Highway, and the Pacific Coast there is a seldom-visited region stretching east from Mt Barney along the Queensland/New South Wales border to the coast at Tweed Heads. Much of this area is high mountain rainforest, but around Killarney the land is more open, with green rolling fields punctuated by sharp peaks.

In fact this is part of the Great Dividing Range, the mountainous backbone of Australia that stretches all the way up the eastern seaboard of the continent. Near Mt Barney there is a pass through the hills leading from the rural areas around Boonah in Queensland over into New South Wales. It is not on a main route, unlike nearby Cunningham's Gap, nor does it lead to any major towns or centres. This makes it a great hidden place and it offers some of the best scenery in this part of Australia.

I last visited this area after decent rain, and I was amazed by the impression of green. Everywhere were green rolling hills and lush fields, and you could almost sense the 'growing' going on all around. It was so striking that I stayed a few days to take some photos – the ones you see here.

Aside from the greenery, there is some drama here too. The Condamine River cuts its way through the highlands, in the process creating Condamine Gorge with cliffs towering over small fields enclosed within the valley. The road follows the creek, crossing it fifteen times at a series of fords, and a four-wheel-drive is recommended.

As an alternative you can drive parallel along the south rim of the gorge past a series of lookouts and end up not far from Killarney village at Queen Mary Falls, one of the highest single-drop falls in Queensland. There are two easy loop walks here and the one to the base of the falls is recommended, especially if the waterfall is running full bore. You may also be lucky enough to see a satin bowerbird and its distinctive blue-strewn nest.

For hardcore bushwalkers, Mt Barney offers challenging treks, but for less energetic folk there are plenty of excellent views and vistas within a few metres of the road.

How to get there: Killarney is 33 km south-east of Warwick. (The region in the photos is to the east of there, along the Condamine Gorge and Wilsons Peak areas.)
Best time: Summer for lush green fields, otherwise all year round is good.
Facilities: Killarney has full facilities, and there is camping at Queen Mary Falls and nearby Koreelah National Park just over the border in New South Wales.
Nearest town: Killarney.
Website: www.walkabout.com.au/AtoZ/K.sthml/

koonchera dunes and
the birdsville track

Koonchera Dunes and the Birdsville Track (SA)

Birdsville is actually in Queensland, but since all but the last 10 km or so of the legendary Birdsville Track are in South Australia it made sense to locate this entry there.

For many years Birdsville was famous for its remoteness and for the gruelling mail route to and from Marree, serviced by horse-drawn buggy until the 1920s. It is still hot, dusty and a long way from anywhere, but the roads have improved and, more importantly, an increasing number of suitable vehicles are being used by visitors to the outback.

Most of the way from Marree, the road passes through vast stretches of scrub country and gibber plains. There is not a lot to see except the road stretching out in front, seemingly disappearing into the heat haze ahead. This may not sound inspiring, but there is one place that makes the dusty trip worthwhile – that is, if you are a little bit adventurous and would like to see some of the best red dunes in the country.

The colour red is symbolic of the Australian outback – the Red Centre is not named that for nothing. Often the sand is covered with spinifex bush or other desert grasses, which tends to mute the effect of large expanses of red. Fortunately there are places scattered around the country here where you can find not only classic bare desert dunes but ones of a stunning deep oxide-red.

My personal favourites are the Koonchera Dunes, about 100 km south of Birdsville, near Goyder Lagoon. You can't see the dunes from the road – this is a genuine hidden place. The Walker Crossing Track, which leads from the Birdsville Track to Innamincka, has only recently been opened to general traffic and is quite rough for the first few kilometres. About 17 km along, look to the left and just on the horizon you will see a red band – this is the dunes system. Since the gibber plain is completely flat at this point, all you have to do is drive off the trail and cross the plain for a kilometre or so.

The dunes stretch off to the left and right as far as the eye can see, but are only about 200 m wide. Each time you go there they will be different, with new ridges and curves forming almost overnight. For the keen photographer, nothing beats bare red dunes with seas of distinct ripples – take plenty of film.

How to get there: Take the Birdsville Track south, turn south-east onto the Walker Crossing Track and follow for about 17 km. Roads are gravel and can be rocky, so this is four-wheel-drive terrain only.

Best time: Summer is too hot and can be dangerous. Please visit here only in the cooler months (April to September).

Facilities: None. Be aware this is a very remote area and visitors should be well equipped and self-sufficient. It would be wise to inform the police at Birdsville that you are travelling in the area.

Nearest town: Birdsville.

leeuwin-naturaliste
national park

Leeuwin-Naturaliste National Park (WA)

The south-west corner of Western Australia is perhaps best known for its great kauri forests and the highly acclaimed wineries of the Margaret River region. It is also home to Leeuwin-Naturaliste National Park, which stretches almost the whole length of the coast from Cape Naturaliste all the way south to Cape Leeuwin and Augusta. The main interruption to the continuity of the national park is at Prevelly where the famous surf break attracts surfers from all over the world and where international competitions are held every year.

The rest of the coastline is wild and dramatic, with stark cliffs continuously pounded by the Indian Ocean swells – which is what makes the surfing at Prevelly so good. Some of the cliffs near Willyabrup and Cowaramup offer challenging rock climbing for the more adventurous.

To the north of the park are more spectacular rock formations, the most striking of which is the complex of channels and rocky outcrops that make up Canal Rocks, just south of Yallingup. A natural 'canal' separates the main rocky spur from a small island and there is a wooden bridge conveniently placed there for visitors to cross. It is possible to spend hours watching the facinating ebb and flow of the swell as it spills in over the ragged rocks and then sucks back out in ceaseless motion.

If beaches are your thing, then just outside the national park are the amazing azure coves along the coastline from Eagle Bay to Dunsborough. The colours of the Indian Ocean are quite distinct from those of the Pacific on the east side of the continent: the blue water is subtly more turquoise and the vivid white sand accentuates its colours.

Inland, the kauri forests soar over a lovely scenic route from the Margaret River village south to Hamelin Bay and Augusta. The main highway misses most of this forest, so take the extra time and follow the slightly longer minor road as it winds through the lofty stands of trees.

The Leeuwin-Naturaliste region is a place where you could easily spend a week exploring the various coves and forest trails. As with many of the places mentioned in this book, getting off the beaten track can lead you to some lovely hidden places.

How to get there: Margaret River is about 270 km south of Perth via Highway 1 to Mandurah and Bunbury, then through Busselton on Highway 10.

Best time: It's a Mediterranean climate – cool and wet in winter but great for the rest of the year.

Facilities: Plenty of hotels and camping grounds in the area.

Nearest towns: Margaret River, Busselton.

Website: www.margaretriver.com

Limestone Coast (SA)

Certain parts of Australia can be seen as complete little packages, offering something for everyone and a great variety of activities and places to visit. The south-east corner of South Australia around Robe, Mt Gambier and Penola is such a region, with great beaches, sleepy fishing villages, top-class wineries and the World Heritage-listed Naracoorte Caves.

All of these attractions sit neatly in an area only 150 km long, just over the border from Victoria and only about 300 km south-east of Adelaide. From Kingston to Port MacDonnell you could easily spend a busy week exploring all that the region has to offer.

Of particular significance is the wine-growing region of the Coonawarra, centred around Penola. Established as a 'fruit colony' by John Riddoch in the nineteenth century, the Coonawarra district has gone on to become one of the best known wine-growing areas in the country, alongside the Hunter Valley, Barossa Valley and Margaret River.

Like other parts of the South Australian coastline, around here it is definitely 'wild and woolly', with jagged headlands enclosing sandy coves and an endless variety of sculpted rock formations created by the incessant pounding of the Southern Ocean against the soft limestone cliffs. When the sun goes down in the winter months it tends to backlight the crashing waves, making the spray glisten with a golden light.

Inland and just to the north of the Coonawarra region lie the caves of Naracoorte. Guided tours are available and the caves are well worth the excursion – the various stalagmite and stalactite formations are some of the best in the country. One looks just like a huge church organ with soaring pipes and multi-tiered keyboards.

Further south, almost at the tip of South Australia, lies the town of Mt Gambier, which is home to the well-documented Blue Lake. This definitely shouldn't be missed – the actual colour is even more intense than it appears in photographs – though for something a little more off the beaten track take the road south of town to Mt Schank, which is also an extinct volcano. Here there's a hiking trail from the car park right to the rim of the crater.

How to get there: Mt Gambier is about 450 km south-east of Adelaide: the roads are excellent and the journey should take about 5 hours.

Best time: Good all through spring, summer and autumn. Grape harvesting is usually in late summer.

Facilities: Plenty of places to stay in Robe, Mt Gambier, Penola, Naracoorte.

Nearest town: Mt Gambier.

Website: www.thelimestonecoast.com

litchfield national park

Litchfield National Park (NT)

Long overshadowed by its more famous relative, Kakadu, Litchfield National Park lies only a modest drive from Darwin and offers at least one feature that Kakadu does not – good, safe swimming holes. Smaller creeks and rock cascades make it hard for the dangerous estuarine crocodiles to move upstream, so places like Buley Rockhole are popular with the locals for a lazy Sunday dip. The delightful series of deep pools is interspersed with small waterfalls flowing over pink rocks, and paperbark trees cast welcome shade from the harsh tropical sun. It's only a few metres from the car park and on a weekday, early in the morning, it is possible to have the whole place to yourself.

Just a few kilometres from Buley Rockhole is one of the park's camping grounds, where a series of steps leads down to the plunge pool below twin Florence Falls. This is another good place for a swim, and you can head out to the falls for a refreshing shower under the cascading water. Both Buley Rockhole and Florence Falls are subject to seasonal variations in flow, from a torrent in the Wet to a gentle trickle at the end of the dry season.

Further into the park is the spectacular lookout over Tolmer Falls, where a single plume of water plummets 30 m to a bottle-green pool in a deep chasm. At the beginning of the wet season this waterfall is spectacularly powerful, but it can slow to a more modest flow by the end of the Dry.

If you fancy another refreshing dip, head on to Wangi Falls where there is a very civilised set-up with a small kiosk and easy access to a huge pool. Two waterfalls drop down the pink cliff at the far side of the pool, adding to the splendid vista, and a boardwalk takes you to a platform with a good close-up view of the falls if you don't want to get wet. One other nice little feature here is a natural spa set into the rock only a metre above the base of the left-hand waterfall – just scramble up and you will find a deep pool with room for two.

There is lots more to this park than swimming holes, though. Four-wheel-drive tracks lead to the ancient, dramatically eroded sandstone towers known as the Lost City (not to be confused with the two other Northern Territory rock formations of the same name) and more remote parts of the park. All in all, Litchfield is worthy of at least three days to fully explore its nooks and crannies as well as taking time out to enjoy the most peaceful spots.

How to get there: You can enter the park via the bitumen road from Batchelor on the Stuart Highway, about 100 km south-west of Darwin.

Best time: April to October. Access is generally limited during the Wet (December to March).

Facilities: Excellent camping grounds, both park-run and commercial (these are outside the park).

Nearest town: Batchelor.

Website: www.nt.gov.au/nreta/parks

mimosa rocks
national park

Mimosa Rocks National Park (NSW)

This is another example of how following the main roads can take you past some sensational places without your knowing it. South of Sydney, the Princes Highway generally follows the coast, but near Narooma the road cuts inland to Bega before meeting the coast again near Merimbula. There is a minor road which follows the coast instead, and if you take this rather than the main highway you will come across the little-known Mimosa Rocks National Park.

The park is split into various sections, with much of the land having been donated by private citizens to save it from development. The main part of the park follows the coast and includes some great rock inlets as well as a couple of gorgeous beaches.

The northern section of the park is where the Mimosa Rocks – named after a ship wrecked here in 1863 – are to be found, and there are numerous bushy campsites provided so you can stay right near the beach. The little bay near the campground has a 'bouldery' beach, and at dawn the warm oranges and yellows of the rounded rocks, together with the smooth hiss of the breaking waves, makes a gentle counterpoint to the stark outline of the rocky pyramid beyond.

A little further south is Middle Beach, which offers some good surfing breaks and a long stretch of golden sand. Even better is Moon Bay, slightly further south again, where a short walk takes you to a tiny sandy beach squeezed between two rocky headlands. The water here is a deep turquoise and, being sheltered from the worst of the ocean swells, it is crystal-clear.

There are plenty of camping grounds along this stretch of coastline, mostly tucked away among the trees. There is also plenty of wildlife to enjoy and it is not unusual to wake to the sound of kangaroos munching on the grass outside your tent. Here at least, nature does not wait for the alarm clock and a cup of coffee before going about the day's business.

How to get there: Mimosa Rocks National Park is 413 km south of Sydney.
Follow the coast road from Bermagui to Tathra – the park is signposted.

Best time: All year round, but winter can be cool and wet.

Facilities: Basic camping in the park, with toilets but no water.

Nearest Town: Tathra.

Website: www.nationalparks.nsw.gov.au

mitchell plateau

Mitchell Plateau (WA)

The Kimberley region of Western Australia is often described in travel brochures as a 'last frontier'. It is definitely a long way from anywhere and the roads are generally only suitable for rugged vehicles. I think this puts off a lot of people, which is a pity because the Kimberley offers such a variety of scenery and experiences that it is well worth the effort to get there. More and more tour operators are offering high-quality tours in comfortable vehicles and you can even fly in from Broome or Kununurra.

The Mitchell Plateau is right at the northern end of the Kimberley and over 100 000 hectares have recently been set aside as Mitchell River National Park, including the main drawcard to the area, Mitchell Falls.

The falls in full flow are one of the grandest sights in the country. The roar of the four individual falls is tremendous and the cascading water forms endlessly fascinating swirls and eddies as it dashes down to the pool below. Even the one-hour walk from the carpark is interesting, although care must be taken to follow the trail.

But the Mitchell Plateau is not just about scenery. It is also one of the most historically significant parts of Australia, with a continuous timeline of Aboriginal occupation going back tens of thousands of years. Rock art abounds and the sharp-eyed visitor will see many striking examples of the Wandjina figures, or rain spirits, painted under rock overhangs.

This region is also home to countless examples of rock art collectively known as the Bradshaw paintings, named after their discoverer William Bradshaw, who stumbled upon them in the 1890s. Little is known about these paintings, which feature slender, animated figures and are believed by some experts to predate the Wandjina paintings by thousands of years.

Wandjina images are scattered throughout the Kimberley, many on private land and many as yet unseen by outsiders. Some of the more accessible ones can be found around the King Edward River, close to where the track to Mitchell Falls crosses the creek. There is an excellent campground here and it is worth breaking your journey at this spot to enjoy the cool pools in the river and to explore.

How to get there: Mitchell Falls are accessed off the Kalumbaru Road, 172 km from the Gibb River Road junction, 240 km from Kununurra.

Best time: Roads are closed during the wet season (approximately December–March). So aim to be there early in the dry, around April when the falls are at their best and the roads have opened.

Facilities: Camping ground with toilets but no other facilities. Campers should be fully self-sufficient.

Nearest Town: Kununurra.

Website: www.calm.wa.gov.au

moreton island

Moreton Island (QLD)

Just like its famous big sister to the north, Fraser Island, Moreton Island is a sand island with freshwater lakes, coastal heathland and vast dunes. Unlike Fraser Island it is only a short ferry ride away from Brisbane, making it an ideal destination if you don't want to travel too far.

Despite its proximity to the state capital, Moreton still offers vast stretches of open beach and the opportunity to sit back and enjoy the sensation of being a million miles from the rest of the busy world. With most people flocking to Fraser Island instead, Moreton is one of southern Queensland's best-kept secrets.

To enjoy the sandy beaches and crystal-clear waters you really need a four-wheel-drive vehicle, since all the roads outside Tangalooma (the main resort, on the west coast) are simple sand tracks and the eastern beach is the road on that side of the island. It is possible to hire suitable vehicles fully equipped for camping and there are a number of operators in the city who can kit you out.

One of the best spots on the island is Honeymoon Bay at North Point, just to the west of the Cape Moreton lighthouse. The white sand and blue water are like something out of a travel brochure, but the images are quite genuine – the water really is that blue. There is good fishing, swimming and a decent surfing break, and during the quieter parts of the year it is still possible to have this place all to yourself.

The eastern beach is a great place to pitch a tent, with small camping areas tucked away in the dunes between the she-oaks. There are plenty of gutters along the beach for fishing and in the early morning light it is quite common to see solitary fishermen in bright waterproofs standing in the rollers.

If your preference is for the peaceful bay side of the island there are also fixed campsites along the shore north of Tangalooma, which are completely sheltered from the ocean swell and so are great places for families.

As well as camping, fishing, and swimming in the sea you can take a dip in the Blue Lagoon, one of the island's many 'perched lakes' (which occur above the water table).

How to get there: By ferry from Scarborough or Brisbane River. Once there you can only get around via four-wheel-drive or on a tour.

Best time: Lovely all year round.

Facilities: Bush camping along the eastern ocean beach, with full resort facilities at Tangalooma.

Nearest town: Brisbane.

Website: www.epa.qld.gov.au and www.tangalooma.com

orpheus island

Orpheus Island (QLD)

Dotted along the north Queensland coast are innumerable islands, from tiny sandy cays to huge tropical settlements like Hinchinbrook. Some are national parks, some are uninhabited and some, like Orpheus Island, have full resort facilities for visitors.

Orpheus is situated just 25 km off the coast north of Townsville and is part of the Palm Island group, which also includes Pelorus Island, Fantome Island and Great Palm Island. The islands are all surrounded by inshore coral reefs, so there is snorkelling directly off-shore and long deserted beaches to enjoy.

Great Palm Island is home to an Aboriginal community and as such cannot be visited without a permit. Fantome Island is uninhabited but can be visited by boat and has superb beaches and an old leper colony (established by Sir Raphael Cilento in 1939) to explore.

Orpheus Island has some delightful spots. One of the best is Yank's Jetty to the south-west of the island, not far from Fantome Island. The sturdy jetty is publicly accessible (by boat, of course), and there are small camping spots scattered around behind the beach area. Take a small boat across from Taylors Beach near Ingham and spend the night at Yank's Jetty or one of the other campsites for a quintessential 'desert island' experience.

For the (very) well-heeled, the Orpheus Island Resort on the west coast offers five-star facilities in an idyllic and sophisticated setting, perfect for some serious relaxation. All meals and activities are included in the tariff, and with a maximum of forty-two guests you know the beach will not be crowded.

James Cook University operates a very well-equipped research station, also on the western coast, where scientists stay in bunkhouses. The state-of-the-art facilities, being so close to the Barrier Reef, offer some superb opportunities to add to our knowledge of how the delicate ecosystems work. It is possible to visit the station by prior appointment and, if you are prepared to offer your services as a volunteer, you can even stay there. Accommodation is clean and new but basic, and you have to bring your own food – but in such a gorgeous location this isn't really too much to ask.

How to get there: By boat from Taylors Beach, 120 km north of Townsville, or by a scenic flight to the Orpheus Island Resort.

Best time: Very benign climate all year round, but January to March are the monsoon months.

Facilities: Camping at Yank's Jetty, Pioneer Bay and South Beach – permits available from the Queenland National Parks and Wildlife Service. Resort accommodation at Orpheus Island Resort.

Nearest town: Ingham.

Website: www.epa.qld.gov.au or www.orpheus.com.au

otway peninsula

Otway Peninsula (VIC)

The Great Ocean Road and the Twelve Apostles are firmly entrenched as favourite destinations for visitors to Victoria. This is a fabulous spot and thoroughly deserving of its popularity, but don't neglect the lesser-travelled hinterland.

Melbourne is not far away, so the temptation is to take a day trip to see the main sights and then head back to the city. What many people don't realise is that just inland from the Great Ocean Road is the huge Great Otway National Park, covering over 100 000 hectares and encompassing Otway National Park and Angahook-Lorne, Carlisle and Melba Gully State Parks. The area has a network of roads and picnic areas, and you can see superb temperate rainforest and literally hundreds of waterfalls.

The best time to enjoy the rainforest is during cloudy weather, especially after rain. The greens of the forest canopy are at their most vivid and, of course, the waterfalls are likely to be in full flow. Overcast conditions also make for the best photographs. I know many people are disappointed with the photos they take of rainforests: this is because the contrast is too high when the sun is shining – the leaves are bright, the shadows are deep and film cannot reproduce the true sense of lush green that your eyes experience. Shooting in overcast conditions minimises the contrast and allows you to capture the depth and texture of the forest. So if it clouds over (which is not unlikely given Victoria's notoriously changeable weather), head inland a few kilometres and enjoy the rainforest in optimal conditions.

The Aire Valley trail is a good place to start, where there is a well defined route starting just south of Lavers Hill and leading through the trees to Beech Forest. Along the way you will see stands of colossal Californian redwoods planted decades ago. These vast trees are an incongruous sight, since not only are they massive but they form their own microhabitat of open understorey, which is quite different to the tangled and almost impenetrable native forest.

Just south of Beech Forest are the Hopetoun Falls. This is one of those places that many people have seen in photographs but not been sure exactly where it is. Not only is it a classic waterfall but it is also at the end of a very pleasant walk through the densely packed tree ferns that form dark tunnels, muffling the sound of your footsteps.

Hopetoun is just one of many waterfalls that you can easily visit. Others include Beauchamp Falls, Erskine Falls, Sabine Falls and Stevensons Falls.

How to get there: Apollo Bay is central to the area and is about 180 km south-west of Melbourne.

Best time: Access all year round, but best in the summer as winters can be wet and cold.

Facilities: All local towns have full facilities, including camping grounds, fuel, etc.

Nearest towns: Apollo Bay, Lorne, Princetown.

Website: www.parkweb.vic.gov.au (downloadable park brochures).

snowy river national park

Snowy River National Park (VIC)

The Snowy River conjures up images of high-country cattlemen, lakes, and hydroelectric power stations. That is the other end of the Snowy River: this national park is much further downstream, where the river is wide and flows strongly towards the coast near Orbost.

This part of East Gippsland mostly consists of hills covered in dry forests, with cypress pines and white box. It contrasts with the wetter forests to the north and east, where the genuine high country is often covered in snow during the winter months. The area was settled by Europeans first in the 1840s by farmers looking for pastures; and later (the 1890s), by miners looking for silver. The 15-km Silver Mine Walking Trail explores this aspect of the area's heritage.

The river flows through a series of deep valleys, and within the park it can be followed via narrow winding dirt roads passing first over McKillops Bridge and then south along Tulloch Ard Road. This road is quite safe, but it is narrow and large vehicles need to take care on the sharp corners.

While there is good camping around McKillops Bridge, the best spot for those with a four-wheel-drive is at the bottom of a short trail to the west of the bridge – it's marked on the park maps. The camp sits right next to the junction of the Little River and the Snowy. During the short time I was there I saw dozens of azure kingfishers, and spotted two platypuses in the pools at the riverside. Across the water there was a group of wallabies – too far away for me to be sure, but they may have been the rare brush-tailed rock wallaby which lives in the area.

The easiest access to the river is in the southern section of the park, not far from Buchan, at Balley Hooley Campground. There is a lovely grassy camping area, with picnic tables and toilets, beside the river which here flows through a series of rocky outcrops. This would be a great place to bring a canoe, indulge in a spot of fishing or just picnic by the river on a hot day.

How to get there: The park is 450 km east of Melbourne. You can get there via Buchan from the south or via Delegate River from the north-east.

Best time: Summer. Winter is harsh and the river is often flowing fiercely.

Facilities: Basic camping in the park, with toilets but no water.

Nearest towns: Buchan, Orbost, Lakes Entrance.

Website: www.parkweb.vic.gov.au

stanley and the north-west

Stanley and the north-west (TAS)

The north-west coast of Tasmania is one of the most fertile parts of the state, its rich agricultural land perfect for dairy and beef cattle, and crops. The coast is also very scenic, with distinctive headlands breaking the expanses of long quiet beaches.

Of particular note is the oddly shaped formation at Stanley known as the Nut, which is made from basalt (rock cooled from volcanic action ages ago). The rock is extremely hard and has resisted weathering to form a very distinct plug erupting from the relatively flat surrounds. The feature's name is derived from the local Aboriginal word – *Moo-nut-re-ker*. Looking back east towards the Nut from the stone ruins near Highfield House, one is reminded of a sperm whale swimming past with its high forehead and back protruding from the water.

A sand spit connects the Nut to the mainland and on both sides of the spit are long graceful beaches. Huddled at the base of the basalt cliffs is the small town of Stanley, which has managed to retain some of its original charm, with brightly painted weatherboard houses and shops keeping the town in character.

East of Stanley, just inland from Wynyard, is the unusual waterfall known as Guide Falls. A basalt ledge has formed a hard edge for the creek water to flow over and, since it resists erosion, mosses and lichens have been able to gain a foothold on the rock itself. The overall effect is of water cascading over a green velvet cushion. There is a peaceful picnic area about 100 m from the falls and it is a pleasant place to stop for lunch.

Not far from Wynyard is another distinctive headland, Table Cape. Bigger than the Nut, this cape towers over the Bass Strait and you can look straight down from the white lighthouse to the clear waters below. Rich farmland extends out onto the headland and in spring you can see rows and rows of tulips growing in multicoloured ranks – quite a sight and one worth timing your trip for.

How to get there: Stanley is about 130 km west of Devonport.

Best time: Spring through to autumn. Winter is cold and can be wet. Weather is very changeable, so bring warm clothes!

Facilities: Places to stay at Stanley (excellent camping ground and cabins), Wynyard and Burnie.

Nearest towns: Stanley, Wynyard, Burnie.

Website: www.tourtasmania.com/nw

tarra bulga national park

Tarra Bulga National Park (VIC)

Deep in the heart of Gippsland, well away from main highways and cities, there is a landscape of huge mountain ashes, ancient tree ferns in lush gullies, and vast gnarled myrtle beeches. Tarra Bulga National Park is a section of the Strzelecki Ranges that was set aside in 1903 to save the area from being cleared by settlers. The first reservation, of 20 hectares, was named Bulga, from the Aboriginal word for mountains; the second large section (303 hectares) added five years later was named after Count Strzelecki's Aboriginal guide, Charlie Tarra. Hence Tarra Bulga National Park.

This whole region is characterised by rolling, steep hills with tall ash and blackwood trees on the slopes and deep fern-lined gullies in between, forming an area of cool temperate rainforest typical of the southern Gippsland highlands. The moist cool conditions make a very good growing environment for tree ferns, and forty-one species have been identified within the park.

The Tarra Valley Road from Yarram, one of the least known scenic routes around, gently winds along ridges, over creeks and through stands of thick rainforest, each bend promising a new vista to enjoy.

In the park there is a visitor centre with maps of all the walking trails – of which there are plenty. To see the best variety of scenery, follow the Wills Track from the Bulga car park, cross Corrigan's suspension bridge and loop back via the scenic path and Fern Gully Nature Walk. Make sure you look down from the bridge because you'll see a vast sea of tree ferns – viewed from above, the massed ferns appear as a series of interlocking circles.

The other paths lead through the ash forest, where you can see evidence of early logging in the form of huge tree stumps. It is amazing to think that these giants were felled using hand saws and brute force, not to mention the difficulty of taking the logs out through this dense vegetation.

This is a haven for wildlife and whilst you may not see the denizens of the understorey, you certainly can hear them. The eastern whipbird has a very distinctive call, and the familiar songs of kookaburras and currawongs add to the noisy atmosphere. The park is also home to the superb lyrebird, and numerous marsupials including wombats, gliders and possums.

Rainforests can be quite hard to photograph, but this particular park, with its winding access road, could have been custom-made for the purpose. The combination of the straight trunks of the massive ash trees and the fascinating patterns of the tree-fern crowns just cries out to be photographed, and I was only too happy to oblige.

How to get there: Tarra Bulga is 220 km south-east of Melbourne. Follow the Traralgon Creek Road south from Traralgon on the Princes Highway or north from Yarram along the scenic Tarra Valley Road.

Best time: Accessible all year round, but cold and wet in winter.

Facilities: No camping within the park, but there are picnic areas at the Visitor Centre and the Bulga carpark.

Nearest towns: Yarram to the south and Traralgon to the north.

Website: www.parkvic.gov.au (downloadable park brochure).

umbrawarra gorge
nature park

Umbrawarra Gorge Nature Park (NT)

Just south of Pine Creek, between Darwin and Katherine, a turnoff on the main road leads to Umbrawarra Gorge, a lovely little canyon of pink rocks through which flows a small creek. It is a great place to stop off for a bit of an explore; there is even a small camping ground near where the creek crosses the road, with enough space for about half a dozen tents.

From the parking area a walking trail leads along the left bank of the creek and before long the rocky walls start to loom overhead. After a kilometre, the track peters out at a golden sandy beach opposite a huge rock wall with turrets just like a fantasy castle. During the early dry season, from about late March onwards, the creek will be flowing and this is a good spot for a cooling swim and a picnic. By the end of the Dry the creek will most likely have stopped flowing, but the waterholes usually stay full. Opposite the beach is a small Aboriginal art site – you can see small arrows drawn under a rocky overhang about 3 metres up the rockface. The more adventurous can scramble up to the left where, overlooking the second pool just around the corner, is a large overhang with more paintings on the back wall. If you are lucky you may even see some of the local marsupials – short-eared rock wallabies and rock ringtailed possums live here in significant numbers.

Adventurous walkers will also enjoy rock-hopping and wading further down the gorge, where it narrows and deepens. Past the abrupt bend is a sheer-sided wall over a deep pool with another sandy beach, beyond which the gorge opens out a bit though it remains very pleasant and quiet.

Umbrawarra Gorge is a classic hidden place, as it's very easy to miss even though it is marked on the maps. With the little camping ground and great swimming holes, it is a good place to break a long trip and get some exercise exploring the rocky depths of the gorge. It is at its best at the beginning of the Dry, but is still worth a look even at the end of the season.

How to get there: Three km south of Pine Creek, take the Umbrawarra Gorge turnoff to the west and follow the road for 22 km.

Best time: March to October – the earlier the better, as the creek stops flowing late in the season.

Facilities: Bush camping only.

Nearest town: Pine Creek.

Website: www.nt.gov.au/nreta/parks

warrumbungle
national park

Warrumbungle National Park (NSW)

If wildlife and bushwalking are your thing, then the Warrumbungle National Park, just outside Coonabarabran in central New South Wales, is the place for you.

The park is based around a remarkable series of volcanic outcrops and ancient vents that form the huge rock pyramids known as the Warrumbungles, the most striking feature of which is the towering, wafer-thin outcrop of the Breadknife. Seen from the park's Visitor Centre the skyline looks impressive enough, but by following the well-marked trails you can walk amongst these fascinating rock formations, which are much bigger close-up than they seem from a distance.

The Breadknife, in particular, holds some surprises. The trail up to it starts off paved and sloping gently – and you think 'This isn't so bad'. Then it gradually steepens, still paved, and your legs start to feel the strain. Soon you reach a series of beautifully constructed steps, which seem to go on forever; they take you to the base of the Breadknife. There is a narrow break in the rock wall and if you carefully enter it the world seems to drop away, since the other side of the thin rock wall is several hundred metres lower than the side you are standing on.

A few hundred metres further on, and up, you will come to the Grand High Tops with a 360° view of the valley, the rock spires, and the Siding Springs Observatory to the east. The whole loop walk is 12.5 km and quite strenuous, but thoroughly recommended. It should take about 4–5 hours.

The wildlife in the park is as spectacular as the scenery. There are few places in Australia where you will see so many eastern grey kangaroos as around the park headquarters and campground. You're most likely to see them if you find yourself driving the local roads at dawn or dusk, as they are unafraid of cars but can be wary of two-legged visitors. The park is also home to Australia's other favourite marsupial, the koala. Keep your eyes open and scan the forks in the trailside trees along Spirey Creek and you will be rewarded with glimpses of little furry bundles fast asleep in precarious spots high above the ground. It is a joy to see these animals in the wild – most people only ever see them in wildlife parks.

Apart from the plethora of furry creatures, the park is also home to 180 bird species, including king parrots, swift parrots, turquoise parrots, emus and wedge-tailed eagles.

How to get there: The Warrumbungles are nearly 500 km north-west of Sydney.
You'll find the park 35 km west of Coonabarabran, on the John Renshaw Parkway.
Best time: All year round, though it can be frosty in winter.
Facilities: Excellent camping ground, with hot showers, barbecues, etc.
Nearest town: Coonabarabran.
Website: www.nationalparks.nsw.gov.au

western macdonnell
national park

Western MacDonnell National Park (NT)

Alice Springs makes a great place to start exploring the famous Red Centre of Australia. Within a short drive there are plenty of places to enjoy, such as Simpsons Gap and Standley Chasm, but being close to town these spots can be a little crowded, so it is well worth the effort to head a bit further out and deeper into the Western MacDonnell National Park. Along the way you will see the deep-red rocks for which the region is so well known, scattered with pure-white ghost gums that stand out brilliantly against the harsh, rusty escarpments on either side of the road.

Follow Namatjira Drive which, beyond Standley Chasm, splits off from the road that leads to Hermannsburg and takes you past a series of delightful rocky gorges. Each of these has good swimming spots, places to picnic in the shade, and walking trails for the more energetic. Ormiston Gorge is a good example, with well-made trails leading down to a creek bed which usually has pools left over from previous rain. Paperbark trees lean over the water and in the distance the huge bulk of the MacDonnell Ranges looms over everything.

Ormiston Gorge also sits right on the Larapinta Trail, which links all the good spots in the park, all the way from the Old Telegraph Station in Alice Springs to Mt Sonder near Glen Helen. The 223-km trail is broken up into manageable sections which each can be traversed in a day and offers superb views.

At Glen Helen, an exposed rocky escarpment is split by a narrow opening through which the ancient Finke River occasionally flows. There is a small motel and restaurant here, which makes it a good base to explore the surrounding area. Best of all, if you get up early, the red cliffs above the river burn red-hot in the morning sun.

A little further out from Glen Helen the road reverts to gravel, but if you have a four-wheel-drive it is a good idea to make the short trip out to Redbank Gorge, a narrow slot canyon guarded by a chilly pool. Take an airbed to paddle about on and you can have a great time exploring a short way into the canyon.

How to get there: Follow Larapinta Drive west out of Alice Springs and turn right when you reach Namatjira Drive (after about 47 km).

Best time: April to October, since the summer months can be intensely hot.

Facilities: Accommodation at Glen Helen, and camping at Ormiston Gorge with showers and barbecues.

Nearest town: Alice Springs.

Website: www.nt.gov.au/nreta/parks

william bay national park

William Bay National Park (WA)

Of all the coastlines in Australia, the section around Albany, Denmark and Walpole in the south of Western Australia must surely rate as one of the best. In particular, if you enjoy sheltered azure water and interesting boulder formations, then William Bay National Park should be on your list of places to visit.

Situated just a few kilometres west of the township of Denmark, William Bay National Park is centred around the twin beaches of Green Pool and Elephant Rocks.

Green Pool is a couple of minutes' walk from a small car park and on reaching a platform at the bottom of some steps you will be greeted by classic Wetsern Australian views. Friendly-looking rounded boulders seem to float in the calm turquoise water and to the right the beach seems to stretch away to infinity.

The boulders shelter the main pool from the ocean swell and the overall effect is more like a man-made swimming pool than a natural part of the generally rocky coastline, with the clear water and bright sunshine creating shimmering and shifting patterns on the white sandy sea-bed. If you take the trouble to wait until late afternoon, the sun sets over Point Hillier in the west and the colours reflect off the surf as it surges in over the boulders. A lovely spot for an evening beer or a glass of local wine.

Just to the east of Green Pool, over a short rocky spur, is another beach at the base of a short inlet. Here, the friendly boulders of Green Pool have morphed into huge rounded shapes that burst out of the water, reminiscent of elephants bathing in the sea – hence the name Elephant Rocks.

This is a great place to scramble around and there are interesting rock formations to explore on the eastern side of the inlet. The white sand emphasises the blue of the water, making it almost painfully vivid, and the weathered, rounded rocks complement the overall palette of colours.

How to get there: William Bay National Park is 10 km west of Denmark and some 400 km south of Perth.

Best time: Any time, although winters tend to be cool and wet.

Facilities: No facilities at the park except toilets. Camping and accommodation in Denmark.

Nearest towns: Denmark and Albany.

Website: www.calm.wa.gov.au

william creek
and lake eyre

William Creek and Lake Eyre (SA)

William Creek is really just a single pub, hardly a town at all. There is an airstrip there, and a phone box, but it's basically a watering hole in the middle of nowhere. It's on the Oodnadatta Track, which runs from Marree up to the main Stuart Highway via the township of Oodnadatta. It is also very close to Lake Eyre, Australia's legendary inland sea, and has thus become quite a busy spot, especially when the lake is in flood.

The pub oozes outback character. The last time I visited, there were thousands of banknotes from all over the world tacked to the ceiling, people had written their names on the walls, and there were business cards pinned to every other space. Each year they hold the William Creek Race Day, which seems to consist entirely of drinking games on the Saturday followed by some actual horse races on the Sunday.

Lake Eyre is Australia's largest lake system and since the rivers from all around flow into this huge geological depression, early explorers were convinced there must be an inland sea at the heart of the continent. In some respects they were right, but the rivers only flow strongly enough to reach the lake every few years, so the 'inland sea' is usually a waterless, pale-brown salty expanse stretching as far as the eye can see.

However, when it rains and the rivers flow, Lake Eyre is transformed. Wading birds from who knows how far away congregate in their hundreds of thousands. Banded stilts, pelicans and gulls form huge flocks as they trawl the shallow waters feeding on tiny shrimps that emerge from the mud like magic.

Word gets out quickly, and within weeks the little settlement of William Creek becomes a haven for groups of visitors from all over the country looking to experience spectacular scenes of the lake in flood. The local aircraft charter company puts on extra flights and they carry parties over the lake from dawn till dusk. Flying is the best way to take in the lake in all its glory – especially at dawn when the colours of the early morning sky are reflected in the utterly still waters.

It is possible to visit the lake shore, either at the Lake Eyre South lookout on the main Oodnadatta Track or by following a trail from William Creek to the main lake's edge. The latter route is remote and rugged, so make sure you tell the publican that you are going there.

How to get there: William Creek is 405 km north-west of Marree, which is about 700 km north of Adelaide. The road from Marree is a dirt highway that is well maintained but can be dusty with some corrugations.

Best time: Summer is definitely too hot. Best time is April to September.

Facilities: Camping or basic cabins at William Creek.

Nearest Towns: William Creek, Marree.

Website: www.williamcreekhotel.net.au

wilson's promontory

Wilson's Promontory (VIC)

Wilson's Promontory, or 'The Prom' as it is also known, is a popular tourist destination, but its distance from Melbourne (around three hours' drive) and the need to book to ensure your accommodation (a ballot is used to allocate campsites in summer) means it has remained a special coastal wilderness.

The area is rich in flora, ranging from temperate rainforest through coastal dunes and heathlands to stands of white mangrove (the southernmost mangrove community in the world). There are some 30 species of native land mammal to look out for, including rare creatures such as the swamp antechinus. Other significant residents include a small damselfly, a 'living fossil' once thought to be extinct but sometimes encountered around freshwater lagoons.

This national park contains superb beaches, peaceful creeks, spectacular rocky headlands and some quite serious overnight bushwalks. Most of the park is undeveloped and only part of the west coast is accessible by road, as far as Tidal River and Mt Oberon. The rest is left untouched and if you want to see it then the only option is to walk.

Tidal River is the heart of the Prom, and tends to be packed out during peak season. The short walks around here are very popular, so for more hidden pleasures aim to do one or more of the longer (day or overnight) hikes – to the lighthouse, for example, which offers overnight accommodation – or explore the wilderness area in the northern section. There's a rewarding day walk from Darby Saddle, a little north of Tidal River, along a mainly uphill coastal track to the headland known as Tongue Point. Along the way, take the detour to Fairy Cove, a secluded jewel accessible only at low tide.

Outside the high season is a good time to visit since you will be able to find a campsite without too much trouble. The staff are aware that many people from outside the area will not know that the park is often full, and a small number of sites are reserved for such visitors – very considerate, I thought, but do ring ahead to check when you go.

How to get there: The Prom is 200 km south-east of Melbourne. Head for Foster: the route is well signposted.

Best time: Accessible all year round, but often cold and windy in winter.

Facilities: Excellent facilities including fuel, general store, visitor centre and large campground.

Nearest town: Foster, Fish Creek.

Website: www.parkweb.vic.gov.au (downloadable park brochure).

yarra ranges
national park

Yarra Ranges National Park (VIC)

The Yarra River and Yarra Valley are reasonably familiar destinations, but you could miss the little town of Marysville if you stick to the Maroondah Highway.

Getting to Marysville from Melbourne involves the dramatic drive over the rugged yet lush Black Spur. Marysville is less than 100 km from Melbourne but seems a world apart from the bustle of the big city. Oak trees line the main street and in autumn the whole town blazes with gold. Winter brings snow to the nearby mountaintops and at Lake Mountain (only 22km away) there is an alpine lodge, toboggan runs and cross-country ski trails.

In the summer this area is favoured by bushwalkers: the high-country trails lead through stands of snow gums and the views from the various lookouts are splendid. In fact, with Melbourne being so close you can probably see most of the way there – should you want to. Personally I prefer to look away from the big city and towards other parts of the Yarra Ranges National Park, which are in stark contrast to both the city and the alpine region.

Very near Marysville are Steavenson Falls and the valley of the Steavenson River, which is filled with classic temperate rainforest. There are tree ferns everywhere and lofty ash trees soar overhead. Further out is the old logging settlement of Cambarville where more of this verdant, ancient forest is to be seen – particularly at Cora Lynn Falls where every tree is covered in lichens and mosses, tree ferns provide a silent canopy to walk beneath, and you feel you should talk in whispers.

Back in town there is another delightful excursion along Lady Talbot Drive, which follows the Taggarty River as it burbles over big mossy boulders, sheltered beneath giant ash trees, twisted myrtles and the ever-present tree fern. This is a place where, to coin a phrase, time stands still. It is easy to imagine that this forest has remained unchanged over millions of years, and without visitor impact would be unchanged for another million. Along the way are numerous small picnic grounds, so you can often find one all to yourself.

How to get there: Around 90 km north-east of Melbourne. Follow the Maroondah Highway to just beyond Coldstream and take the turnoff to Marysville at Narbethong.

Best time: All year, with the added pleasure of snow in winter.

Facilities: Full facilities in Marysville.

Nearest Town: Marysville.

Website: www.parkweb.vic.gov.au (downloadable brochure).

Acknowledgements

I would like to thank the Northern Territory Tourism Commission and the Fourwheel Drive Hire Co. for their assistance with my Northern Territory shoot, and Fujifilm Australia for their ongoing support.

I would also like to thank my wife Janelle for her assistance on all my photographic trips.

PENGUIN BOOKS

Published by the Penguin Group
Penguin Group (Australia)
250 Camberwell Road, Camberwell, Victoria 3124, Australia
(a division of Pearson Australia Group Pty Ltd)

New York   Toronto   London   Dublin   New Delhi   Auckland   Johannesburg

Penguin Books Ltd, Registered Offices: 80 Strand, London, WC2R 0RL, England

First published by Penguin Group (Australia), 2006

10 9 8 7 6 5 4 3 2 1

Cover and text design by Elizabeth Theodosiadis © Penguin Group (Australia)
Australia map based on original by Demien Demaj
Typeset in Sabon by J&M Typesetting, Melbourne
Printed in China by Everbest Printing Co. Ltd

Cataloguing information for this title is available from the National Library of Australia

ISBN-13: 978 0 670 02988 4
ISBN-10: 0 670 02988 2

www.penguin.com.au

Note: The maps in this book show approximate locations only